michael magee

SPUYTEN DUYVIL

New York City

Spuyten Duyvil
PO Box 1852
Cathedral Station
NYC 10025
1-800-886-5304
http://spuytenduyvil.net

Acknowledgements: versions of some of these works were first published in *Callaloo, canwehaveourballback, Cello Entry, Combo, CrossConnect, DC Poetry, Ixnay, Kenning, Kiosk, Lungfull!, Magazine Cypress, Mirage #4 Period(ical), Open Letter, Shampoo,* and *Skanky Possum.* Thanks to all involved.

Some of the poems here were published in the chapbook *Leave the Light On* by Boog Lit (2000). Thanks to David Kirschenbaum and Aaron Keilly. "Trading Fours" was written with Nate Chinen on email, antiphonally: the odd stanzas are mine, the evens his. Thanks to John Parker for permission to borrow his email for "Prolegomenon for the Black Irish."

Thanks to Bill Berkson, Jessica Chiu, Jacques Debrot, Kristen Gallagher, Michael Gizzi, Kevin Killian, Susanna Magee, Carl Martin, K. Silem Mohammad and John Parker for their responses to the work.

for my family

and in memory of Rachel Raffler

What, in the head, goes wrong—
the circuit suddenly
charged with contraries,
and time only is left.
                    –Robert Creeley

I mean it's hard since all we have is our dialects, our ways with words
and the rhythms of our saying; sometimes when we think we don't
know what we mean we find out what we do mean, language is like
that. The meaning is saying.
          This is the difference between blues and despair.
                    –Charles Bernstein

Bah! Depestre the poem is not a mill for
grinding sugar cane absolutely not
and if rhymes are flies on ponds
                              without rhymes
            for a whole season
away from ponds
                              under my persuasion
let's laugh drink and escape like slaves.
                    –Aimé Césaire, "The Verb 'Marroner'
                    / for René Depestre, Haitian Poet"

CONTENTS

LEAVE THE LIGHT ON

The Brain, within its Groove
Runs evenly – and true –
But let a Splinter swerve –
'Twere easier for You –

To put a Current back –
When Floods have slit the Hills –
And scooped a Turnpike for Themselves –
And trodden out the Mills –

—Emily Dickinson

EASY COME, EASY GO, EASY DOES IT

nature makes water
on your parade

I'm the virus in your papyrus

suppression is a tactic
as milk is lactic
this is a fact check
from the girl at the hat check with a hatchet

think how trees feel from
the back of the bark
fly-papered against the
                                gypsymoth rumors
now the moths
now the paper   gypsies

a pack a lips don't make a kiss
as five balled fingers a fist

elementary, my deer thought so

paint your
phantom limbs   against
                 the weather

gum up the works, service your dentures
on a dented fender in the wilderness, surrounded
          the junkyard
                dog rained
                          on by other
dogs (you) and
cats (me) and   vice versa

so that's me, girl, and you, inside and out
don't let stub a door jamb on
the way   root for your nerves

LEAVE THE LIGHT ON

there is sunlight, many photographs and some text.

                    —Bill Berkson

if this is a rainbow I've missed a lot
the test for color blindness involves
hidden numbers   .   hidden numbers
and a small red cap moved variously

it's marginally interesting that "shaft"
can be both vaginal and phallic
don't you agree? there's a remake
of *Shaft* in the works and I wonder

whether this might be incorporated.
the proverbial pot of gold. color
blindness, of course, primarily affects
men. to shaft someone is decidedly
masculine, as to fuck someone over,
but one who *gets* the shaft is of indeter-

minate gender. we all, after all,
have more orifices—shafts—than
you can shake a shaft at. and
more than one woman, no doubt,
has given a man the shaft, the
pre-verbial pot o' gold if ever there was
a leprechaun w/ 2 1/2 vaginas & 2 1/2 penises.

Creeley gets away
with a lot of what
would otherwise
be male look-
ing at "a hairy /
hole" b/c we sense
the fractured "sub-
ject placed / by the
verb" the "unhappy
in its / circum-
stances" & suspect
he may be merely

somehow checking
out his own

        but did he ever run with her —
standing up — "through a rich moist
shaft that is caving in" as Berkson
in "Rebecca Cutlet"— now that's
a trick!

            what is a rainbow to
the colorblind, or, am I un-
      manned by my central
                              scatoma?
lost w/out my
military gaze?   Look: eyes
                are not penises

hell, *penises* are barely penises under
certain conditions, go ask a
leprechaun…no, wait, you
better let me go first

at the end there was a bright
in the navel of a knight
at the other end, your leprechaun
of the sort to wean a skeptic on

all's back projection in the
theater of thrice folded sausage links
reticulate, retinal, sensitive, jest

"Our eyebeams twisted, and did thread"

pour us a porous soft drink in our
porphyritic torpor, said these
two to the bartender
                    all's ventriloquy
in the ass-pants of a Renaissance has-been

        men don't get it, says my dentist
            well I do, says I
        it's unusual, says he
            un-who-sual? ax'd me

must viruses invade the nerves
thus to disturb our metaphoric paraffins;
are they the necessary anti-generic angels,
the leprechauns even in Stevens' underpants?

Richard Pryor, Annette Funicello & I
are related on our syndrome's side
all things run together in the prismatic
spin cycle
             and a small red cap
moves variously along the blindspot

A CASE OF NERVES

treading water oh so negativo to
the swimming composition

a flutterback in the rib, the
skull skulling —

      briefing the candles, the mouth bothers

gives out, takes
                in the
                equilibrious sticks
          bone rattle
     as in
a cat's nasal
        purr

the rest of the brain is barley
                  chubby in
the soup, not a grain of truth in a
wicked pittle-pot for the piebald-rotten
fishcroppers, as the invented snot
once spake it this
              the emergency anglophone
plot's me exit, eh red?

once outside, I le'go me ego
though me id be toast'n me
host be hid
            knuckles, collar-
bone, pelvis, patella, elbows,
jaw, tendons, heart, valves, flutter-fist

TALK TO YOUR KIDS!

that's where flowers come from, Freddy.
the business of the wetter the knot the
funkier the root is a half-truth blessed in
Clotho's crib after hours: bleed at if you

want. benighted we banned debreeded
we ball and that's where flowers come
from. the fields are strained thru a gold
filter, dear, the rods assembled by a

small staff. the weather is one determining,
termed a factor. the e is silent. a
festive occasion winds up in the blotter for
batter a horse. why is a question of motives.

when you were young we dropped a bedlamite
into your parapets. the flowers blo-
omed quite accidentally. howdy pilgrim
soul. we loved that about you, your hidden

face. but understanding is the wicked, one-
legged step-cousin of decision — no
doubt they had your number even then, wise
to the ways of the index, since the days when

the thumb was a tumor. two more days. bitterness
as usual. there are some who will draw your
attention to the crop circles. note their cauliflower
ear and, if you must, hang your hat on another cornucopia.

the hills are alive with Gucci pylons:
we-in-the-business meet those-in-the-know

on the bathroom floor of the
icy internet café latte intolerant

a nor'eastah rains out the party
politics in Mighty Mouse's trousers: they

beg to differ, beseech your lordship
lollipop in the hobbieshop, horse

sense dictating, boss, the codes of
our best peoples: where's all this

aggression coming from? if wizened
veterans collect hoarfrost, *why, oh,*

why can't I? in word-sized hail
I'm all back that up bluebird, hand

in the blockbuster late return slot
and while the egg on my face is my

own ovum, and morning is known as Dawn
so don't *I* do donuts, Don: on your front lawn

EVEN STEVENS

does rancid meat pass
the test of time? speak low,
for I've inquiries regarding
rancid meat   .   if the
guts of the bus are the eyes
of the bee holder   no use
disputing the net, or
the rancid meat it once
kept: handsome as you, heft
heav'nward, it hung; until,
stunk to high heaven, it
descended .   the rise of
rancid meat, the gist of myth
reached proportions
in high minds   .   lies in the
unfortunate fridge
a different tradition. the
cots apron if a kicked
sheet is an appropriate
replacement for a
bowl of fruit   .   rancid
meat with faux pineapple
filling   .   between the land-
lord and the lampost   "for
the birds"   the scythe of time
to make the donuts
drives thru .   what you
make of it, this product

FRAGMENTS FOR JOHN PARKER

the package arrived in Berlin
you were in Tulsa
this seemed appropriate

does Marxism, then, require the
existence of God?
a question I'd been meaning to ask you

my nerves are shot — a bleak joke
I'd been meaning
to make

self-deprecate: pray against oneself
depreciate: lessen the value or price of

somewhere here is a joke for you

the brain, I read today, continues to
grow into old age
what grows *out of* old age?

I think maybe we should restart
our dialogues — but from
Berlin, another place I've never

visited, like Mars

"for you were called to freedom,
brothers & sisters, only do not use your
freedom as an opportunity for self-
indulgence, but through love become
slaves to one another"

need your comment on this

I think about getting well a lot
I think about getting, well, *a lot*

my lot in life, one's lease on life
funny phrases

Death, maybe, isn't gluttonous, as in Donne—
it's more like, someone says to Him, "You
want the rest of this cheeseburger?" and He
                    says, "I guess so."

but pain
is earthbound, you bet; a good thing too, or else

doctors like him are great stoics I can't help
but admire
                 they've seen a lot more shit
than most, which probably counts
for something

"only bodies exist, all else is subsistent [*huphestos*]"

how does that square?

so, God, yes, in their case, but
as *active material*, "an inside job"

"God makes 'em, God takes 'em"
– my dad

a totally
insufficient thing
to say
                  except perhaps in
                  context: as response
to the body
gone ass-backwards
for no known reason: "it just does that"
the rhetoric of what's appropriate
a needle or a ray, concrete, prepositionless

LIVING DEAD

for Nathaniel Mackey

On the evening of November 5th
like King Oliver (*c.f.* "Call of the Freaks") with
Albert Ayler took the ferry
out dixieland's constraints — but very
to the Statue of Liberty
near: the *transition* fertily
and jumped off as
hatched in old cadences:
the boat neared Liberty Island
the slurred "wor'd without end"
On November 25th his body was
or cause cousin to "*'cause*, cuz"
found floating in the East River
the limb, even when severed
at the foot of Congress
survives as prayer for redress
Street Pier in Brooklyn
or in the orphan one took in
"My blood has got to be shed
"a child will lead," he may have said
to save my mother and my brother"
"another" — or, earlier, this other:
as one in/with the unrhymed line:
"If I'ma break the rules, I'ma learn em"
the way to a man's heart is through his sternum

BODY OF THOUGHT

you and your
dirty mind or
me and mine
where does it
       end?
end?
   does this hurt

does this hurt

     does this hurt

know to weighs around it, the matter
behind
   space is the place
   you hear *whoa-oh heave ho*
that's
history, which has nothing to do with this?
when
   company comes
   misery gets all exciited

weaning the
curse of human
avants

   you
are the code
leader

   on the fly
's wings they've
writ

   the code
   the order, "sheet
stuff" you
know?
        you know. me?– I
        'm – no, no –

I

don't *need* a bio
hazard, I *am*
       a
biohazard, ad
-vancing in play (!)
                          other-wise
waning or adroitly loitering–
                         can you
believe that?
no words
        worthian
        high resolution   on the
                                    horizon or

la la
        la la

meant of such: out
on a limb
        a drip
bagged – like, packed

AUT(O IMM)UmN(E)

there is definitely a way in a witch
october afternoons the macabre body
does its job, shivers me timbers
all hellos even break loose   its tea

time in the pantheistic pants of the Aztec
artifact collectors   .   they do it right
greasing the tree surgeons before they leaves—colorful

wicked index numbness   run down   worry wart
symptom accelerant dreamt—
vertiginous jaunt, the minds joint account
waiting, fly, the soup   .
                              yourself *in* yourself
                              sad [see SATURATE]
in the unmaking, able   .   .
y'all bring me them nine-knotted orange fishnets,
some cobbler. . . and Red Foxx   .   .

the wizened Wittgensteinian feels his pain in
your foot   .   let me look at those clammy cells
just as I suspected: o'er-brimm'd   .

the gadblasted wind aloofly woos the synapse
don't rock the boat, as Ma says, especially
if there's urine in it. she's dreary, that one

injectables and pins, a role in the hay, a
stacked deck   .   he left with the
hat check girl, melting in digest form

R

my purview ain't too nosy
it was after
I met John
that r's entered
my vocabulary, "like a thief in the night"

now I want to cry in my
puppy dish of inscrutables, no offense

is there *really* a porcelain god?
he said nervous like

condition means so many
things in this
here culture

beginning in the carnivorous
period, we traipsed out of Nordstroms
"as a people"
                    the food court rift and
                              squirrel burger a
theorized paradigm
shift

some of us died, the allergic, the Good,
the asthmatic, the One, not
to put too fine a point on it

my epidermis is fuzzy, you know?

go figures
in
                    to a morphine taper
when you're a
when your courtier's
the close cousin of a proper tapeworm

fuckem what say *I doubt not
't will be over by eventide*, and fuck

                you if you
                say it
outside of language the most natural things
are the upwardly mobile maggots spilling
over
        the lip
of my green plastic trashcan

inside of language it's me
hoseflooding them streetwise

                the body has a mind
                of its own which is out
                of its mind, mind you,
                and a part of the body

like when we got hosed streetwise, remember?

something's brewin' in those moonlit puddles
looking back   the house
            is glowing   as with
aliens or
several TVs   or them worms

as when someone says, I'm thinking it's the transmission

EARLY BIRD'S WORM

anything, a cornut apéritif, a palliative
the bathwater ominous in the ear
the rosy char of deflation, apical
in the nape

      forget catastrophic
      haplogroup insurance
      better Cheddar (fitter)
      luck o' the pyre
sdrawkcab ssa
against the warpthread granule

wrung number / dumb waiter / opposably thumbed

nosiness breeds

all feet all   river
feet all feet   dabbbed   mouth
              tissue

all permeable fumblerooski for keeps

    who left the breath-
    taking fiat on the floor?
                   we warble
      "always talking" as
spot arcs
the x   makes a spouse a ledge
a held thresh
    aching watermark

BODY SHOP

I believe we may have an opening
a do-it machine in our achy breaky botanica
Encyclamenia, I bleed at there's an opening for you
lead us not into temping stations
but deliver odds and ends to people
in the old cyclonic raft riff: bereft rift
you know a good
                          body shop for detail work?
we often arrive with shit in our mouths — we're shards
real chrono-nos midst exempli
gratia proverbs a la six of NAFTA
half a dozen of NAMBLA; I mean, six of mutual-
ly assured destruction, half a dozen mothers
against drunk driving
                          When the alarm
went off
we had an alarm reaction — welcome
to the club!

[3]It is precisely at this moment under these circumstances that
Window Theory breaks down: hearthside, the glass jaw shatters
in the draught; the abcess of theory has eased them asses but
each of own is primed for the Hitchcockian rope-a-dope.

you should have received this in your packet
right in your packet

when, undrawing the blinds, it is one of those
"Truths universally acknowledged" that some
light visits of an uneclipsed morn
man, man mans the window
closed, it can fill, be scaled to, centered on,
or tile the screen
open, the screen heard in the distance
thins membranous
                          you're free to go
      through
guided   by a thread   of violets

SPRING & SOME
       for Michael Gizzi

penurious chill, sun out   sun's out
on the parch   what's that
expression – the girls
         to come by?
more delusions
than a syphilitic Franklin?
        no thanks, ma'am
atomic
cat, atomic bird
             vernal bugaboos
      the buds
    marked: FRAGILE

3) mid-summer: don a
   downy chapeau, mister sex comedy

 plant this

   dig my snug pen
(that's
   penis, Seamus)
         (and that's me
         buttercup you
      just fucked up
   wise acre)

I'm a Gerber daisy, baby,
but I grow like a weed

BLACK IRISH:
A GRAINY AMERICAN DREAM

*Is it any wonder ivory hunters are
music lovers or that black Irish
are often black?*

> –Michael Gizzi

Your Irish skin looks Mexican

> –The Pixies

GRAINY AMERICAN DREAM

if we don't do it
someone else will

that's Italian!

as spaghetti & meatballs
Leonardo DiCaprio
and fascism — and:
cowboys

dead animals, dried
plants, & plastic
outfitted

going something like — what? —
a *million* mph?

it's called orbitting — ever heard of it? (far out)

somnambulant and sweaty
dream in which drone in dromos
drinks dram while
playing drum

it's known as dramaturgy, dummy!
said the little Italian girl

just because I'm in
the dummy pass, that don't
make me a dummy *per se*

said her black Irish suitor

uh-huh, an just because I got
Cap'n John Smith's dick in me
that don't mean I'm Pocahuntus

said the object
of his affection

being thus left to our fortunes, it fortuned
that within ten days, scarce ten
among us could either go or well stand,
such extreme weakness and sickness oppressed us

I see

it's like "Caught Sleeping" meets "One Explosive Lap
Dance"

where were
we? We?

the hardest thing
to say, impos-
sible

that's Italian!

we will say so

"you"
"are in an unconverted state"
"and so are aliens"
"God seems now to be hastily"
"brought in now"
"without being thrown down"
"arbitrary"
"We find it easy"
"what are we"
"the hand of"
"every unconverted man"
"laid in the"
"wise man? even as the fool"

"Natural"
"hell on a"
"bottomless"
"born again"
"a stage for your"
"fly open"

"the creation groans"
"it came as a thief: Death outwitted me"
"a foundation for the"
"rotten covering"
"flatters himself in"
"the numbers"
"healthy constitution"
"always exposed to sudden unexpected"
"brimstone"
"experiences"
"in the covenant of"
"Application"
"easily broken in pieces"
"and so are aliens"

PROLEGOMENON FOR THE BLACK IRISH

if I'm back, where
does that leave my back

after big MacAttack
the rhythm sprung and attract me

Dear Madam,
        Will you please let this
white boy have some books
by Richard Wright?

I give my self / the back of my hand

lighten up, black Irish
                        eat them potatoes
            the food of your peoples

speaking of: Sharon, I says, you can
stay
            right here
                        I says
you don't have to go nowheres
she says but I don't got no money I says
you go with Christine
                        to bottling plant tomarra
I says you stay right here till your on your feet

                        money talks, bullshit
                        talks back
                        through a walkie-talkie
as the saying goes
you go with it

            club feet & all
            with a club to a
            club, neanderthal
            hath thee in thrall

that's reaction-
                    ary on four levels, mister
                              allegory

the "I'm Tiger
Woods, motherfucker!" of indecision
the bathroom (P)ledge in your House of Pain—
                              don't jump!

when I was a lad, me mum would
whisper me stories of Robbie Caruso
and the royal wee

                    on good Friday
especially we
loved the middle passsage
about the fishwife of Montserrat (late of Cork) who married a moorcock

birthed a monkey and named him "Burnt Norton"

Alas, although the law is universal, the majority live
as if they had understanding peculiar to themselves

mum said

Well, if you think the Norton anthology is bad, try the Laurence Welk show. I
just caught a rerun which featured a very peculiar routine: a group of brightly
clad white people on what appeared to be mock bleachers, all holding basket-
balls, sway gently to the sound of "Sweet Georgia Brown." Half-way through a
black man dribbles on stage, tosses his ball to the bleachers and begins a tap rou-
tine. This culminates with the white people bursting into song, carrying the
lyrics of Sweet Georgia Brown in four part harmony as the tapper taps up and
down the center steps of the mock bleachers. For the grand finale, he dashes
down the steps, drops to his knees with his arms spread wide, smiling to the
camera, and the chorus behind him begins in unison to *pelt* him with their bas-
ketballs, as he draws in his arms and craddles his head, cringing. Then cut to
Laurence who says, I swear to God, "Well I hope you have enjoyed our colorful
show." -jp

a gd pt you have there, john   .   member the
                                           dismembered busing
                                           tablaturers—

complicit commitments
riotous conscription—

the wooden floor's expansion

can we start at the very beginning (rasa taboo) when it ain't trane's
      favorite?

(before the face)
         as if

Hæc loca, vi quondam et vasta convulsa ruina
Dissiluisse ferunt, cum protinusutraque tellas
Una foret

taint already
a colonized language   .   .

spectral shells run the gamut's grave stone
so much for gravitas scaling the majority
Do you know a quaint, lax *re*ason,
Fibber? *Mira:* gestimate *family*
tutorials, *so*lve pollution, *la*bile reality,
sanction John's *ti*ny hymnal, do*do*bird.

Tap the Ballinskelligs at a snail's pace
sans cargo. *Segrue* carved in granite,
subject to Cromwellian erasure, granted
(or the sea's shell game + T = analogous
accomplishment)
           the Kinsale gourmet
butters up history, cleans and seals loose
indentures. How describe the passage w/
out conflating the middle, black ire-ish? after
the Celts game on Causeway, the pub's bumper
sticker—*top o' the mornin' to yo' ass*—marks
the rivalrous anxiety of the bleecher creatures

Banister, a wild Irishman…a fellow of absolute barb-
arity…forcibly took Caesar, and had him carried to the same post
where he was whipped…told him he should die like a dog…

look kids—big Behn, parliament   .   what'd you
                                   say your
                                   Surinam was, Brutus?

giving it to Caesar, as w/ Cranchal later (bro-love)
bad blood spread by mosquito (n. ask k gallagher abt
                                        fishtown fever)

*

don't call it a comeback vs. comeback, baby

reading Reading reading Reading
they shit in his bed not a word in
his bed Reading bed not a word
trashed his place in sheeps clo-
thing *pick up the pieces* lachrymal
Cousy might have said lachrymal
Cousy might have did lachrymal
Cousy might have, yes, but Cous
came tumbling after: block block
black block block black block bl-
ack alone in reading's trenches

*

Leprechaun in the Hood (2000, Horror)
Warwick Davis, Ice-T.
Aspiring rap stars unleash an evil leprechaun's fury.

*

BEHIND THE LACE CURTAIN
                        for Patrick Herron

"a dash of"

scotch dashed on the rocks
like Fat Albert on Prince Albert: like
school on Saturdays: no class

Magee, Jacob. Sampson, NC. Moved to Miss.
Magee, Preston. Pvt, 148th Vol. Infantry, Co K. PA, 1862.
Magee, Jackson. 10 U.S. Col'd H. Art'y (REFERENCE CARD:
original filed under: Black)

that's history

"ancestral matrix…as the French say,
entre les deux"

                              where's my Scotch?
          you "wild Irishman"

come out from behind there with your back turned
                              you colorful pensioneer

keeping up with Joneses   getting Jonesed

those are some pro cons mister Tar Heel Baby

          Sonny! I'm stuck—get
                              me a

                    bandaid

nah, man, I ain't got nothin
to do
                    with you

Sample the scampy drivel of court wits in an alienation

Uncle Mike is in the house
"Sir Willful Witwoud, is in the house"
a grievous con brought
                              to you
               by the maker
's of "2 Caliban Sam & the Gang"
and the *naturally tempestuous* flavor of Frosted Humps™

THE LAST DAYS OF FREEDOM

I was well aware of all the prejudices of the people
against machinery & of their notions about the extortions
of Bakers, Butchers, &c., which notions, Corruption's press

was constantly fostering; but I know my countrymen well–
I knew that, if in kind language they could be made
to see their error, they would no longer persist in it

& I relied on my own talents to produce that conviction
in their minds. A word about their minds: served fresh daily,
the tenderest of them harbored no ill will toward even

the beggars-can't-be-choosers in the remote constituencies.
& who could execute a verbal joust in such unphobic
quarters? Verily, one spent no less than a third of one's

time fingering the last olive in the jar. & more verily than
that I can't fathom. Windward, a storm cloud,
conjured as occasion saw fit, chomped at the bit. The

hounds were spooked. The candlestickmaker's empty panes
shattered. I stumped for calm, recalled for skeptics
the vestigial tails of wellwishers, made contacts for

their mind's eye &, peeling their onions, produced tears.
The machinery cowered in bleak overhead compartments,
poor darlings. I flanked plebian notions with asthmatic

scares – unkind? One might protest and bear witness
to such were not the extortions of so precise a nature
as to exclude all thoughts of my entanglement. My

countrymen know me as a banquet crooner & hearth
stoker – & well they might. We censored broadsides
by tablature alone, found foster homes for orphans,

served fritters to veterans. All pleasantries are duly
noted in the annals as in the ventricles, vesicles &,
yea, tentacles & testicles. Our errors are quite to our

credit I made sure to tell them. The machinery's
forgiveness is boundless, unintelligible, wet, & warm.

PALE FACE (1)

wet matches in Natchez
Amygism takes a holiday
Jelvus borrows money
or:

        "write a more narrative version and
        see what happens"

wait in the wiggle room; eight in the weightroom
ate with the bridegroom
Carolina BBQ, burnt cork
went to chu'ch. . . the end

beggin strips don't bacon make
donuts break for Grease Monkey
w/ Sherman's dixiecrat Trust in the tank
we all three
of us prayed to the bank sprinklers
cussed in the dustbowl, fingerdipped and signed the cross
what gave you the right

let me give you a visual: pudding
do-over seer bites flag
applies vanishing cream, as seen
in the pictures, hides
                in 94% fag-free closet
            camp boots its cookies
topsy-turvy, the dipshit's Kings beat the dealer's blackjack

PALE FACE (2): BEFORE SPELLBINDING, REMOVE PROTECTIVE QUOTING

what we told you
was true

version trumps aversion
white flight is hard work opening its garage door

the blood on the tips of bootstraps props
the window in springtime,   the better
to view   hummingbirds w/out glaring reflection

discrete vacations clear the minds tawdry vacuum bag

in those days your angelic dimples
were stacked as a balm planted weekly
at the finest markets, "by them shelves," as
                                        the boy put it

birthweight still binds us
the foyer is a heritage museum
your tidewater cousin (removed)   is a gauche

but necessary shelter covers wagers with ivy

open the door little policy major
ChemLawn saves lives

THE FARMER AND THE COWMAN SHOULD BE FRIENDS!

for Kevin Killian

My name's twice when I was what
Wilbur wasn't. Don't get me wrong.
Eyeball it and tell me you wouldn't
Elbow ere Ana wobble 't on a
Cowbell of the jarhead Will. The dragon
Fly's a wallflower to the shit. The shit
Flies like the crow. The crow's an artifact.
My, my, fan the fire, admitted. Well, well.
Mind if it signals your burro, compadre?
Blind stubbornness filibusters my right
Queer notions. Let's burn a subsidy masked as a
Near elegy under the stars, piss in front of the Big
Bear. Ain't sentimental if it ain't continental.
Kind as kinfolk drifters & regular as droughts and drafts.

DAUGHTERS OF THE AMERICAN REVOLUTION

wessson you mean like smith's wesson that's her
daddy what is
like a gun for a penis no like what
black guys use you mean her daddy's black guy's penis is a gun
what are you a sicko he owns it
but that don't make it right
what are you a bleeder he leases it
but that don't make it kosher what are you
an internationalist that company's as red white and blue
as anybody's underpants you mean her dad's a
safety lock
what does that have to do with law enforecement what does this
have to do with Daughters of the American Revolution
because its her god given right
because she own it in the vagina
what
because it's reproducible like a big production I believe you
are finally telling the truth at last
and he was corking up all along I'm not privy to that
and he was corking her up on occasion I wouldn't put in that
light say something about protection
always use protection no no about firearms always protect
your fire arm
you're goddamn right (long pause) can I ask you something
can your mama ask your daddy something well okay what
about all that oil they sell that's a different
company altogether like what you call mixed company when
you really mean
vaginas right and that must be what all the oils for
you dumb idiot now listen *oil* gold for
cooking and black for driving and heat and one giant
of a man of the world of today to sell sell sell
like you was gonna deep fry mother earth herself in it you mean
like her daddy's black guy's penis is a gun hell yes it's a gun but
it's long as a hanging rope and thick as a tree ain't
you been listening

Dear P.,

I know of two nursery rhymes that deal with the subject
of urination. They are, in the order in which I heard
them as a child, "Michael, Michael motorcycle, turn the
key and watch him pee," and "Me Chinese, me play joke, me
put pee-pee in your Coke." The first seems to me a
Cronenbergian fantasy/nightmare which could very easily be
as old as the motorcycle itself, or very nearly so (on
second thought, not quite so old as Gottlieb Daimler's
gasoline motor-powered bicycle of 1865 but more likely at
some later date when the motorcycle became a viable form
a transportation — 1880 — and an iconic product in/of
consumer culture — around WW I, that first war in which
men and machines are gnarled together and, incidentally,
motorcycles were used to transport secret messages), and
which responds to the anxiety over automated transportion
(are we becoming so "attached" to our machines that we
will cease to be able to distinguish ourselves from
them?) by either displacing that anxiety onto an "other"
— the "Michael" in question — who becomes an object of
derision; or, conversely, by *fetishising* that "Michael"
as a sort of exotic, futuristic specimen.

Distinguishing between these two modes of operation is
generally a matter of identifying the tone: in the
former, the rhyme is spoken in cadences of anger and
disgust; the tone of the latter, meanwhile, is so gleeful
as to almost prevent clarity of diction, and the lines
may be repeated several times — so that on occasion a
third party may even need to intervene.

As for the second example, I'd say it is the product of
three related social vectors:

1) the bigot's obsession with the grammatical structures

employed by recent immigrants (here too one finds the
strange dialectic: disgust and derision on the one hand,
fascination and pleasure-producing imitation on the other
— though it should be said that such imitation is never
an accurate reflection of immigrant speech but is,
rather, always refracted through the prism of the bigot's
mind; furthermore, it too is a response to anxiety — in
this case the anxiety that his own "English" is in the
process of losing its centrality and, hence, authority.)

2) the old Western myth of the devious Oriental, which is
everywhere, it seems, in Western literature. In the case
before us, it is rendered comical: you'll find similar
characterizations throughout the history of American
cinema — a fairly recent example being "Long Duck Dong"
in the film *Sixteen Candles*, there rendered so ridiculous
as to be not even properly devious but merely
untrustworthy and a nuisance. (For deviousness I would
point you to Fedallah, Ahab's shadowy lieutenant in *Moby
Dick*, drawn by the hand of even so great and generous a
writer as Melville — though it is worth mentioning that
Melville includes within his text the possibility that
Fedallah is in fact *imaginary* and so anticipates the very
critique at which I am presently gesturing. In any event,
I would refer you to Said's *Orientalism* for a
comprehensive discussion of this vector, which, I think
you'll find, also includes within its logic the various
tropes of immigration as contagion, epidemic, disease,
"outbreak".)

The Coke. What we have here I think is, again, a
response to anxiety, most likely originating around 1970
with the "opening" of China by Richard Nixon: you'll
recall that this is the same period which produced the
wildly popular "I'd like to buy the world a Coke"
commercials — if this were a poem, I would have broken

the line after "world" to suggest the relationship
between the commercial and the nursery rhyme in question.
The "opening" of China (I refuse to say it without scare
quotes, however hackneyed they may be at this point) is
of course a major event in the rise of global economics,
the effects of which we are still feeling, as the recent
controversies over China's "most favored nation" status
show. Coca-Cola, that most American of drinks, the
nursery rhymer half-consciously suggests is now made in
China (you'll recall that the '70s were also the heyday
of all sorts of MADE IN CHINA, MADE IN TAIWAN, MADE IN
JAPAN jokes, of the Don Rickles variety); and here is
what distinguishes this third vector from the previous
two, namely, its spirit of accuracy: for American
controlled, multi-national corporations had begun to move
their plants and factories to the Third World — to
Central and South America and, yes, to Asia — and, as I
am sure you know, had turned a deaf ear to grievances
regarding working conditions, wages, etc.

Suppose that Coke were made in China: it seems to me
perfectly reasonable to suspect that a Chinese worker (or
a Costa Rican, a Laotian, Pakastani or Venezuelan worker)
might very well urinate into a can of Coca-Cola earmarked
for the United States, at the first possible opportunity.
We should rather ask, by what rational principle could we
expect him not to play this "joke" on "us" who presumed
that, to make him bottle our beverages, one need only
turn the key?

LUCKY SEVENS

then the Norse *canibales* nursed theirs
like nosehairs caught in crosshairs
or tribes in crossfire
everyone pretended to be lost
generating their tails
ain't nobody livin'
in here but us amphibians

felt felt somewhere and not
a swath to feel
felt the hard frictionless pool
table, got a feel for the pool
the temperature skinny dipped
the polar bear club crashed the bar
ordered tattoos for their tits and shrunken nuts

squirreled away in May
splinter for the winter
enter the vendor
in a faith healing contest
and drought management course
and free current lottery
and free rent draft in your calendar

because of the old windows
like old men whistling
dixie from a cracked skull bone
like Hamlet on a ham
radio blowing through
a box of oreos, peering at the flora
in this shopworn story-o

you and I are confederate
one and two are confederate
rubber and glue are confederate
needle and thread are confederate
the quick and the dead are confederate
two and one are confederate
the rope and the gun are confederate

they sold us that conjunction
gave us blinding conjunctivitis
and then didn't invite us
treated us like detritus
like you treat your garden
with pesticides, papaya or papyrus

north to south
mountain to mouth
played high low in the chasm
they interpreted it as a sign
like a welcome mat
for the monkey on the vine, swinging
low over the signifying chasm

                    *

like mallards, like melba
toast we are
dying on the bank
like a bank shot
you can't bank on
like a tanker's tank
of gas   .   thank you

when we finally struck
oil it was just
enough to cover us
like James Dean in *Giant*
we immediately wrote a minstrel
show on the bald heads
of our betters

visions of uber plumes
danced in our fed-exed heads
fried in the barrel scrapes
w/ the leftover barcodes
the estuary in the east
was taken by Christ freaks
who were taken with James Dean, of *East of Eden*

he'd welshed on a bet, gyped
a JAP princess who nigger-lipped some

pop, just like a WOP
they couldn't stop talking stop
talking stop talking, they couldn't
stop talking like they swallowed a WASP
I guess they'll die

I know an old lady
who accentuated her possessives
and fucked her ethnographer
in all of us
I know an old man
he laced eggs with the rotten heart
of all of us

POLITICAL SONG, CONFUSED VOICING

you tongued my battleship!
you bonged my tattle-tale
you maimed my mamby-pamby
Wagnered my Nietzsche
and gotcha'd my sweatshop

there ain't room in heaven for us

you stapled my skeptic
my uptick went septic
you bled on my chopsticks
cropped all my flowers
and bred them for outtakes

there ain't room in heaven for us

poll tested my pontiff
fed chess to my mastiff
smashed half my glass ceilings
you felted our failings
racked, broke and called solids

there ain't room in heaven for us

if Astors passed AFSCME
through ashcan-clad plastics
you'd prob'ly statistic
my dipstick with arsenic
as I blabbed a Catholic
as I fact checked a frat kid
passed out past his GMAT
prepped, tucked and dogmatic

there ain't room in heaven for us

what buckled the vulgate
is good for the frigate
that buffered the big one
pigged out at the picnic
there ain't room in heaven
for fuck 'em with upshot

and there ain't room in heaven for us

a Texas-sized peach fuzz
is hell on the ground blood
a star-struck fetishist
honks for burnt curtains
but you rented my benchmark
you birthmarked my precedent
pressed bets, rolled sevens
packed cherubs for action
you prayed on my carpet
you bombed my parade

and there ain't room in heaven
no there ain't room in heaven
no there ain't room in heaven for us

SAME DIFFERENCE

I feel like a brown bag of miscellany propped against a wall. Against a wall in company with other bags, white, red, yellow. Pour out the contents, and there is discovered a jumble of small things priceless and worthless. . .In your hand is the brown bag. On the ground before you is the jumble it held.

—Zora Neale Hurston

You're between in-between

—Will Alexander

SAME DIFFERENCE

in the imitative phase a grab
bag effect ensues   .   likewise
the rhetoric & rituals

of same — a pizza box and/or
trouser cuffs come hither quality
adheres to objects

bells & whistles
flavor crystals
thorns & thistles

themselves acquisitive little elfin occasions
of one sort or another

try them in your back pockets for godsake, next
to the cross-stitching
                              next to
          the h-e-double-hockeysticks, the
I'm-rubber-and-you're-glue of
pre-prophylactic signification

if squirrels store things
this way then that's what
you are today, you little muffin!

even your melted footprints have been
hoarded, I'm guessing, Mr. Bag-of-tricks!

the snake that crept, the snake that slipped,
the one that slept & walked the equivalent
anthropomorphic lakeside strut, is your wet
whistle, darling, "same difference," as uncle

used to say

when we're under water
when we're in the sky
when we're six feet under
ewes look just like eyes

is that the hook?

are we a cover
group? is that your pain
in my foot? impossible you say to
which
              sentence is
                            the step-
sentence: the imagined
orphan is of some position
in the community.

we're through
to gather
in the corners

the perf'd periphery envisioned
as love, the
                    imbibing eye imbibed

one's weight soaking wet
in tight-fit permeating permeables
the standard issue, measure

the singular valence as polyvalent in time

a rhythm tongued and
tonguing, taste buds in
the mouth where
they belong while elsewhere

how do you figure
                            between/be twin
the diary queen's lost
pencil fumbled over the goal
line, no

metaphor but a
littoral drowning
and grass-
roots rescue

CONVENTION-AL POEM

we have ourselves
surrounded — come out
w/ our hands where
we can see em?

listening to *Things Fall Apart* pass
2 girls w/ undyed roots & fuckme pumps

some brothers hustle dope, I hustle soap
in the back

      what Amadou to you

later, cable wires in the white poplar
a concrete vector, criss-crossed window
non-apparitional petals to the metal

vassals versus assholes from Vassar
facile as vaseline in a manhole?

now I'm all confused

the belles of St. Mary knell "The Real Slim Shady"
have made up their minds and are keeping their babies
their CHANNELED HISTORY Knickerbocker by proxy

did you forget to program the kith?

if I tell you the kith is self-programming, do I mean

a) kith : kit :: kin : kitchen
b) Knick fans thwart monikers
c) We're born cable-ready
d) Ask your mama

the day-glo (hunter's) orange wallet's got a
heap of Signifyin in it

this item is not available in stores

is this an item
are we an item
you an item, States?
Antietam?

Is History "a fable agreed upon"
or a grumble peed upon

a rumble

hooded Knights' errant nights in the Hood
now available on-line, remotely accomplished

fetch a Signifyin monkey wrench for swinging

meet your accomplice

CONTINGENCY, IRONY AND SOLIDARITY

1

there are some which are
impossible to settle: for
instance, "assless chaps" & "shagging flies"

I should hardly think
so, but
            honesty is the beast's tragedy
as Wilde
should have said in a webcast

if sound   is free
          of grammar   as Or-
nette sa-   id, then

lettuce Goethe unisex
asthma earning esperar, again this guy
lag a patent, either eye's a pontiff's trouble...

murder the fucking pan's what I say

2

I go to askjeeves.com
Next to the cartoon butler, I type

                  Why are there essents rather than nothing?

Jeeves replies: I have found answers
To the following question: Where can I do nothing Online?

This is Jeeves 1ˢᵗ answer to Heidegger's Fundamental Question
As I scroll
Down the
Page thru
Various engines
                  I see

                  The Fundamental Question

O Jeeves

"I admired you from the beginning"!

if Jeeves loves you, if doves leave you
if the Lord above chugalugs your sneaker
then you the man mice spy from the pylon
as a wise man once borrowed my speakers

3

that was me over when and under why
came out from a pile of rakish leaves
outside Marrakech after one Ramadan
and before another, wrote rainchecks

you were orby in the orchard, I lapsed
into slapstick on the ladder's ordinal rungs —
what the hell, the world has Doric column
up its ass, take a number, rummage thru a rumor

amphibian aliens switch hitting in hulls above Atlantis
eat your both/and for breakfast w/ your amphibiotics
mantis-faced visitors spared no change underwater
work for prey to pray for work, but absorbed w/ kosmosis

the sextet plays sextants, raising post-coital shad
in the moonlight, unrecorded among the Spanish
Daggers in the Carolinas: I have covered
this underground lie in spandex, for preserving

TRADING FOURS (with Nate Chinen)

1

okay, to make sonic
logic of phonic plodding
CLASS ACT / CLASS TRIP
the scene, say, Tonic

2

say it: superseding
CLAP TRAP / TAP STEP
with limbic iambics
scenic four to the bar

3

trap door escape hatch
all limbic systems go,
baby, and, as for
bars — the scenic tour

4

seen it all before
(limbs akimbo on the
traps) clapping
jambalaya go-go (where)

5

is a real event —
agreed on the day-old
bread — yet, akimbo: then,
go aiming at something?

6

a greedy pigeon perched
on windowsill a potted
plant falls 5 stories! were
you saying something?

7

ah! pigeon akimbo, I
get it? or've heard
stories anyway. something…
"that were Icarus drowning"

8

made her cry and hard
to live with! "the eyes
like two stones return
straight to earth"

9

straight return, then, this
previous: one sec. of four
as in AABA cry? —
"Ain't Misbehavin'" "Budo" "Body…"

10

& last night atop the World Trade:
"Dancing Queen" (ABBA rears
its ugly & no escape hatch!)   O
budobudobudobudobud

11

& in he walks
as if conjured — the world
worlds, "takes turns in
turning" — a nice trick

12

an ice tray crackles &
"Dusk in Sandi" & eyes
trickle thinking, tinkling
arpeggios. con jobs.

13

when "Dusk in Sandi" becomes
boney "Dust in the Wind"
I'll take the con job —
Three Card Monte on 46th

14

affording stints of phony
stereophonics. what you
see is what. the scenic tour
has deflated oh get up!

15

and get get get
down, or, "get on
up" antiphonal — here's hoping
th'soul *don't* go t'heaven!

16

dishes clichés thunder-
claps. get up on the
downstroke, gripping pen-
nies from you know

17

what, or, who? where
the pennies are from?
gripping Lincoln, Indian Head
they don't buy nothin

18

butting in excuse me
dance a penny for your
tots (tautology: it
will rain tomorrow or...

19

tomorrow or tomorrow: "there
would have been a
time for such a
word...the last syllable"

20

is "bull" — the pose
of Goya's matador is fabled;
at such a time, he's feeble,
lasts as long as he is able

21

and can a dam in eve-
ning seem "long-lasting" merely
in act of contrasting:
bull: matador, bullshit artist

22

cans a crock of it, cracks
a case of mistaken
changes (rattling around in
empty pockets), charges –

23

mistaken duties, a crock attack? —
"Can I have my
pain in your foot?"
Lud Wittgenstein's good question

24

a bastion of sense, anon,
scents: "one is often bewitched
by a word" / "on the other hand a
language-game does change with time"

25

the length to (end) B —
stretching as on/in a break
in a word, A begins *otra vez*
an(other) anon-time is now

26

& now's the time for con-
firmation of phonemes,
phony dreams – sym-
phonic *mise en scenes*

27

funny you mention: rec'vd
today Ayler's Live in GV
his open letter "To Mr.
Jones — I Had A Vision"

28

versions of versification
(alto: SKREEEEECH!!)
on Leonard St. the sex-
tet rages in & out of form

29

four bars and out a
forum of sorts, the new,
maybe, rising at the foot
of Congress St. Pier, Brooklyn

30

re : union — local haunt-
ings, tide lapping at the docks
O sluggish dawn! every morn-
ing making it new

31

O wimperbang! O local key!
dah plodical Sun's determined
re: turn — edabua alba
all about on all fours

32

an off the record concern
with concerted efforts,
concentric circle of fifths
of tonic. yes, have another round

MOTHER MAY I SLEEP WITH DANGER

for Clark Coolidge

as you always say, Juan
most paydirt omwich

to the mistress – or at least
this is the line they fed you

O for a man of ample parts and
"as plain as the alphabet"!

or the inmalapropriate whispers
of the literati, as vernacular

as casual Friday, the Spelling
bee's stinger in your ass. the de-

mocracy of Tori's wigs is the talk
of silicone valets who know

how to pick 'em. at night they
dream of vacations in the stunning ineptitudes

aw, hell, I don't know, Beverly:
try it in what they call

your zip drive! code way lousy
with roosto rulers and a burgeoning

tube top bidniz. an american psycho
behind every viburnum: are those real?

WHAT IS EXPERIMENTAL POETRY, OR,
TEXT MINUS JACQUES' COMIX

well, let me say, I first
discovered it in
the oven, like a bun
with butter pre-inserted
in the center

how did it get in the core, the hard un-
broken surface

                    lacking a fistula?

Nearby, I made
3 concomitant, revelatory observations:

1) if you look at enough shit, you'll find some shit that looks like a lot
of other shit

2) I BLANCA is an anagram for CALIBAN but A BI CLAN is too

3) it's like that movie where the little girl says to Jimmy Stewart, *Look,
daddy: teacher says, every time the bell rings and you smell things, an
a-hole gets those things with which he buys his wings!* And Stewart
looks up elatedly and says, *That's right…that's right!* and you're sposed
to decide whether "Clarence" and Capital are

         a) synonyms   b) homophonic semi-synonyms
         c) quasi-synonyms

[alternate ending]

¶

then, too, there's the issues of my neighbors
the half-white community

                    college students of tomorrow
                    my "or not I" defers
                    to them, the them-en-
tangled me, Sir Houseplant Lawnmow of the
                  Twisted Eyebeams

for when
visual victuals are the

                         poison pill
                         one focus-
es on audio or adios
amigos en los estados unidos, y, hoy en dia, en otra parte

                         mira, mira   "Off the Wall"
                         what's the fairest Victory Tour

¶

if you go around thinking
thinking newspapers

are for starting fires in the family hearth
well, famine artist perhaps the apt

moniker for your inner poet
after all, only TV, movies, rhymes & high fives

are better than the back sections of
newspapers are at personal poetry

              a masturbatory metaphysics of

                         <u>futilism</u>
                         feudalism

is not for those poets who at this hour sing hootenanies to your inner
oppressed hill people or your outer fucked over nurses' aids

         STRIKE!

              against whatever this poet just
              said to you that you thought made you go bullshit

ANOTHER DAY

for Nate Chinen

scratching epaulettes
bestill my beating Bad Business again
best get shiners

three cheers for the downy protégé!
and a chapeau for the promoter!
one more time with *feeling*!
like he needs it!

Rick Tate might be homeless
          seen blowing
on the corner, N. said

"make chaos out of no
longer tenable forms of order"

he did *what* for *what*?

under the skull cap's a skull
under the captain's a hull

would someone please wack the
seven star general with a lampstand?
angelic blowing for unwed moms
dubbed welfare queenism by powers that
busy beeist myths crated to quell

meanwhile the connoisseur butters
our hot crossover buns on the B side
this snot your father sold in Mobile

& RT's sax case like his
noise & O'Hara's heart is open

MISSED EPISTLES

dear sis, your midlife cry hills beans
when i think of you and the others i think of otters
in an oil slick

we are winter people: why do the boys
of summer open our craniums like honeydew
with their wooden bats?

dear bro, your letters disembarked here, forming
the word   snow   pure, driven
I would ask to know your intentions

each flake, they say, is different — how so?
Like a diamond? Like a wound? to lament
its "dirtiness" is to noun its verbs: plowed, melting, driven over

sis, your admonition was amunition for the soul or
fertilizer for the soil of myself, the flower of
your attentions. my petals are, I assure you,

to the metal, nor will they fold or fall
come fowl or fairly high water. fear only
fear itself: I have placed a man at your door

bro there-while-I-am-here, your book
came quite open, a ball of light it was
not, for which thanks. I confess the barbs

cut, — not me but my not-me, my
absence of sympathies, my loves. the man you
dispatched disappeared as readily, my hand was in it

I stumble, sis, on your thesaurus —
Rumplestiltskin was no less dwarfed by Rapunzel
then I am by my leave: your caveat awaits bronzing

another word: am I not unmanned by all this paint?
Time and Talk take taste from these berry juices
Optic begets Scopic, rubbed on, rubbed in

it's a curiousity, dear bro, this gentleman proxy requisitioned
to paint my interiors. he brushed great guns
prior to his dismissal, managing to oil shut an open door

in the process. my house is roofless but a labyrinth
(Amazonian you called it, to unsurprise). my curios bleed theories
and as ever you mistake the water on my floor for discharge

THE COMEDIAN AS THE C WORD

for Carla Harryman

I do not think myself a fright anymore than I do M^r A M^r B and M^r C — yet
If I were a woman I should not like A — B. C.
                    —*John Keats, Letter to Fanny Brawne, August 5-6, 1819*

1. *The Whorled Imagination*

oble: folded over itself, pie in the
face   i am big; you, us—we are
membranous, i.e. we remember our brains
Is this forced a brawny clear cutting
the barracuda's barred heart in a fleshly porpoise
in a school of sharks in waves that were
mustachios, inscrutable hair in an inscrutable world?

epochly inTrusted baton thrusts prove themselves
against the snug hibernal: cold, hard: clean:
the tongue, posed, thrust flat against the
jungle gymnasium, as if unopposed. A saliva
gland pulses like a drum skin, polyphonous, sub-
sonic, as a skinny sailors blush and petticoat
Cloak of China, cap of Spain, boreal mythologies
of maidenhood, the inquisitorial botanists icy
pornorama, multitudinous tones dwindled to one
sound strumming in his ear: short-shanks, short-shanks, short-shanks

overshadowed the extrospective but unwritten
voyager's parasols, chapels, bouquets, under
the faucet of a bath of a separatist's wife's
noncompliance. his dead brain melted in
her like a do, adieu to his dejected manor
the insular nationality of Carolina, miniscule
in the gales, foot-ways of the moon shouldering
the folds of waves, a nonconvocation in an alternate
strain that seemed hallucinating horn, annulled valet

2. *Concerning Vibrations on Landscape and Self-Portrait*

As if raspberry tanagers in palms, high up in
orange air, were not barbarous, nor a savage color,
she, in oracular rockings, left a jar a door . . .

Outside, his violent aggrandizement sought maternal
pangs, his sonorous couplet's nutshells rattling
inwardly, quilled fables of a gold indigenous dew
Rucks took on Scandavian tones, shades of cadaverous
bloom, a necrophiliac rug-cutting in a catechismal dance
She, on voyage in a land of snakes, found his
vicinities had much enlarged and—incredible to
prostrate, divested prudes—did not close her door
Rather, it was invisible, a pillowy mint in her juicily opulent palm
a seed grown fat between opposable thumbs

to her visible and vocable, the speech of
twins, the egotist's gibberish, brushed in dark swaths
making a hole avoiding emptiness or empty fill-
er, shattering ruses of one vast subjugating
final tone, no way resembling his negligible Triton
trumpeting his conch's talon in the solution of half-fish

so much so that emigrant sounds were passed
on as trifles by this Discoverer/Inspector: making notes
he heard a rumbling. the revenge of music papered
itself for later with a claimed mucosa un-
related to climate or tempestuous clarion
in a low glide under and unbeneath the envious
phraseology; a quiet earthquake-style spot of
rosy charm an unfolding blanket of undisclosed grass

free or more than free? gigantic. breath
quavering on the mouths roof, inked on the
toothy balustrades eating grin and riding through

3. *An Approach to Reading Carols*

the book of moonlight was a dual: fiery
loony faggot in history, voluminous sweaty
pilgrimage in changes of deep songs ripening
in endless panicles of panniculus ledges, whisked
off-stage. the morose chiaroscuro, gauntly drawn
continent, and there bipolar, chilled the Law
Leave room, therefore, in that unwritten book

the jaded, sequestered bride penned descants
for her banished melodies, between herself
and her environment: "perverse, wrong as a
divagation to Peking." sea-masked, illusive
circulating in a kith of motives, hymn and flight an evasion

backward lapses. she, the as necessary two-fingered
sun of her desiring, fluctuating between uninhibited
instruments. (He tossed in a juvenile Carolina
of old time, ancient him.) For refreshment, Sally
's vessel's prow out of goblinry, a marked but un-
marketed grind. A lettered against V in crimson
forms rising in the indulgences of laps

came. A regal, palmed juggler, a clownish minimum
epistle to nihilists, color of an iris, annulled dolor
of pink papyrus. vanquished the savoring fetishist
the sacks decaying on the Santa Maria, all adjectives
of the essential prose, so that: river, vessel, rosin
doors, ropes, sacks, ground, dock, not as Being
but, in their warehouse after hours, inhaled

4. *The Idea of a Colon*

nota bene: she bangs the hole abroad
tacking dirty talk, crossing c's and doubting
i's, gets bare, gets laid—by who? with.
Exeunt omnes the colons higher orifice sin Colón
lake laconics reverberations eccentric hymns
concentric irregular circles rippling floral
arrangements bringing aid to cabbages. check
your slack-but-bellicose prolegomena at the
door. rainy day men with tongues to speak
commingled only, rude instances please impeach them-
selves for application, no Eden sapling gum solicitors

melons, peaches, black branches come to bud
husbandry's t & a on a tin pan psaltery or
the banjos categorical gut—the language is
lousy with it. yeast not a bad crop, prick.
clerked experience, the Sepulchral Señor's imaginary

paramor of smart detail, extensive scope: her blood cries
in the landscape: Georgia, the kings daughter; Florida, the vernal puss

the bland cock's excursions, voracious page on
page, exact, misreads the masquerade: folded
coat, glossy buttons, sensitive texts, flourishing sheets

5. *At Home with Shady*

after years having her chits jigged upon a cloudy knee
a hole poked in a sheet, a boy's fangs scrawled
on her cunt by a prickling realist: alert, rebellious
thought embodied but unsymbolized by body, un-
quarted and uncorseted by a rule of thumb. she removed
the digits from her throat in a haphazard denouement
words of the blue infected will stain our syntax
even the true *entangle* makes a snapping turtle of the
body's folds, survives in its own form beyond these changes
a bronzed kumquat harlequined of an *OED*

man long man long prolong quilted lies in a
requisitioned poll. Meanwhile the ructive c
a blubber of tom toms to the tall musicians
grows recreant in the books and to the pages and
profoundest brass. she writes in my nape

"I am the prismy blonde clapped in his hands
the curtains flittered open so do queens
but I'm more often ganged by the cricket players
a silence down and down, and the custodians
(the door was closed) beating their tambours"

a fig and cream for the fig and cream. philosophers
are saps, knaves of thought. fruits laid in their
leaves arose like cracked shutters flung upon the
rumpling bottomness. Outside, the exchequer exposes
his key as if fisc is fistula and fistula is this

6. *With Androgynous Curls*

a bell thrummed. a bold little syllable. music
midwifery of girls opening words unbraided
unbridled, true daughters without signs to the cabin
from her prophetic joint blew a cloudy nee
no rooms, no roof in the social woof and warp
no green fruits in the rhetoric of ripeness, nibbling bidders
eminent anabasis of enfant Napoleans . . .
Avoid sugar, shoot off the divine phylactery strap

weathery rouge in its vermeil capuchin eventual roundness of
pink iconoclast against man-mulctings if not most
sisterly men humbly I'd thirding a thing still flaxen
all din and gobble, blasphemously pink whenever the
lie lacks door-yard for the dull set of affected colonizers
the pearly poetess in gaping earthy aureole and
four more personae: black chromatic vamps improvised on
a pair of vinyl flats, hilarious dark four self
same lights divers and intricate in a double minstrelsy

routed cock doctrine overseas, pruned the stiffest
realist of the family font, stepped in and dropped
the chuckling down his craw. score. (So may the
relation of each man be clipped like the disguised
pronunciamento of John Wayne in after-shining flicks.)
making gulped potions in the obstreperous city, not
doctrinal, invented music came to reciprocal accord
upon out laps, our circles, plain and common things,
shone in the lumens of gorgeous and variable accents

HATS NOODLE

If thought is life
And strength & breath,
And the want
Of thought is death;

Then am I
A happy fly,
If I live,
Or if I die.

–William Blake

Hats Noodle

for Anabella b. 11/8/00

knot   your father's pathogenesis
stranded on

                                                            an Orkney
or a Faeroe   while Pharoah's sideman mines
                              a reedless conch for sound
                    ebbing memory / peach preserves
the daughter who's father demands Dana Farber, the top   notch,
is not
          you   but your mother's patient, her Job   (the O
                              Boston's O, a vow-
el in the moment of trans
                              ition, as in gohoddfahtha   ‿ ⌣
supercilium
grown cilia & cilia

(also lymphing
                              to <u>finish</u>   vanishing when-
ever in New English

                    pack Bonnie's cat in Ovid's yacht
                    wanna make songing of it?

                    Bracken lack a jug
                              Wheelded lock a club
          Taken like a buss
                    Take care t'avoid the forehead

*

and the ford   as all roams lead to road   e.g.
she
greyhounded from San Antonio   after three days she
in Providence she dropped she out she this is not she one
of the she things she that she "just happens"
                              vaya con Viacom, amiga
                    Keep in touch
Buena suerte, hermana

*

       letters sent   *where the dark Housatonic*
                                        winds
                         between Hoosac & Taghkanic
                                                  to the
sea
                        as Irish out as mitochondrial bisque
        and as Misty as broken karaoke
All souls o('e)r(e) to lead   her dad   on arrival
                           Da Boyz   on her arm
                                  Working Reconstruction
                                       over here
in the burnt   out   tap & dye   shitkicker softshoe
across weighstations & antique snowjobs   I'd like to show you
for yourself   a raced history ala Fred Douglass' caulking
                                      struck down
in a space wielding   and covered by yards of snow angel pock-
marks   all boys schools on your key

*

can we speak
                of hockey
        &   mad booty?

                                     Done.
                                     Minstrelsy.
the earth is wound
look: red in the face, bloodshot   blue   .   .

y'a' know mom? Oh, yo no se   .   .

                      these are the turns, the verses in soil, the
terse voilà   a bald bird gathers no mas   open soars
                                         faster
do we the feats "true man" defeat?
imminently, imminently   history is the bad painting in your
good combine
(conversely, seen from
                    space   on living room TV
the earth is painless but the TV is not)
                    a crow in the snow is worth

caw me tomorrow   come home   little syllable

*

conjuring : conjecture ::   where as
injuring : engender ::   as you can see
perjuring : pleasure ::   as I was saying

vast deferrals perfect preferred customers   from snow
the weather outside is frightful
                                        (your bir-
                    th crashed an election, inter-
sected a crook'd sectarian counting
                                        my dooda, my
                                        doubter, my dot
                                        ma debtor, my dada
ditty do dat em-
erging mutter sampler
wailer at mirrors, stager of mere bobs
I
                    won't bore   you w/ blubber analogy   Wait's
                                                mocking
bird   or pretend the impossible embarazo de hombre   is
                                            anything but
                        a pillow, a cloud, an
embarrassed, directionless angel
circulating   .   .   .

<u>Ductus Venosus</u> was believed to have lived around a previous epoch in
prelapsarian splendour, shunting victuals from Placenta to Vena Cava, as
they were then called, all the while circumventing the immature — some
would say uncouth — Liver. These graceful beginnings masked a less
than gratifying future as, having taken the name Ligamentum Venosum,
she withered and, as the narraive goes

Where's the joke

*

all   in the unction   say ahh
                                        fit to be
                                        tied by our own

                                                                sandals
and fired by a hire cause   on purpose   a junked
a popped cork adrift among junkets, —   THE
                                                                   JUNIOR EXECS
                                                                   ❤ BELLY RUBS

                         and sand dollar bikinis

we meanwhile rub our eyes like a genie's   lamp
our limps congenital, baby, like a con's genitals
tho more congenial
                         maybe   depending
                                                   on
                                                   what s/h's in for
"there is always an element of crime   in freedom"
which is why "crimes against humanity" are usually   prefectly
lawful misnomers, incongruous   PARADOX: incongruity is not
                                       healed by order but by an
                                       other incongruity
                                       fire

w/ fire

save yourself   w/ a made of cow   We both have our injections
T-cells by the sea, sure   but we   of all people
        should bury   our last vestiges   of self pity in
light of Joe Oliver's letters to his sister

*

your head smells Beautiful, your butt reeks,   low rank, a
model of Platonism   Fundamental
                                       into that chasm Christianity
        settled down
at the   *same time reinterpreting*
                            the lower as the created
and the higher   *as*
                                   The Creator   This is
                                                          Why people
                                                          Stink to
                                                          High Heaven

(but not why we hit you with the chrism   all that for was
                            the crazy black bottom Irish and the gap
btwn ten sons' "Yule is He" and Joy's "you listen" plus Armstrong's

faux island red leg ancestry, true whenever
                the Pope crams well, shits in the woods or licks his cat
who creeps to the Baptist in us   for his golden drowning

*

someone is always.   putting.   putting the kiss back in Kissinger
bleary about this
                wintry mix out punned panes
                                        rocking
                            asleep
                            you
the melting flake is not a tear or a flake like me, —anymore
than the frost is Frost
                        H2O + crystal
                        Let Coolidge 5 min.
                        "stir 'em up"   *little darling…*

little darling   Kissinger kills babies   sing : singe

                                        fly to the web
                                        and see:

*

protection w/ out protectorate can we?   postpone my
self, hell, the whole   world   anything and everything
                                               anything : everything ::
if it's true
that then   .   .
                    the Pater of defeat dipped in defined whine
                    trains substantial nation

we ride one   to purporters   to supporters
                                                    to porters, pull-
a fast one, man   a body
                                        gets
                    around

in the poplars, the pines,   see cedars historical seceders, oaks in
                                                        Okla's

                                        Nature Theater

do you read me?

                        loud & clear, over
I love you, over   untranslatable babytalk, over   your
                                                      code name
is Senator Dale Bumpers, over   silence, over

and out
and out

*

"we're a winner" or were a winter?
                                          Aunt Tiffany calling
The kith in   from the   Blvd   to the
kitchen
                        We're cooking, and   booking

call us trans for our rants   examine entranced entrances or

sleep the sleep of the dead in a deep deep sled of the
hieroglyph
                                its all rapid this glissade this skillless
                                    glissando
                                    fit & lash flutter, something
written on the body
                drifts   in the literal
                                        path of its co-

mmitment   and dada
                                                    takes position
                                in the
                mobile

November 2000 - March 2001

90